Resignación

NOAH GARCIA
RUDY JUAREZ-PINEDO

EDITED BY DIANA JAUREZ

Table Of Contents

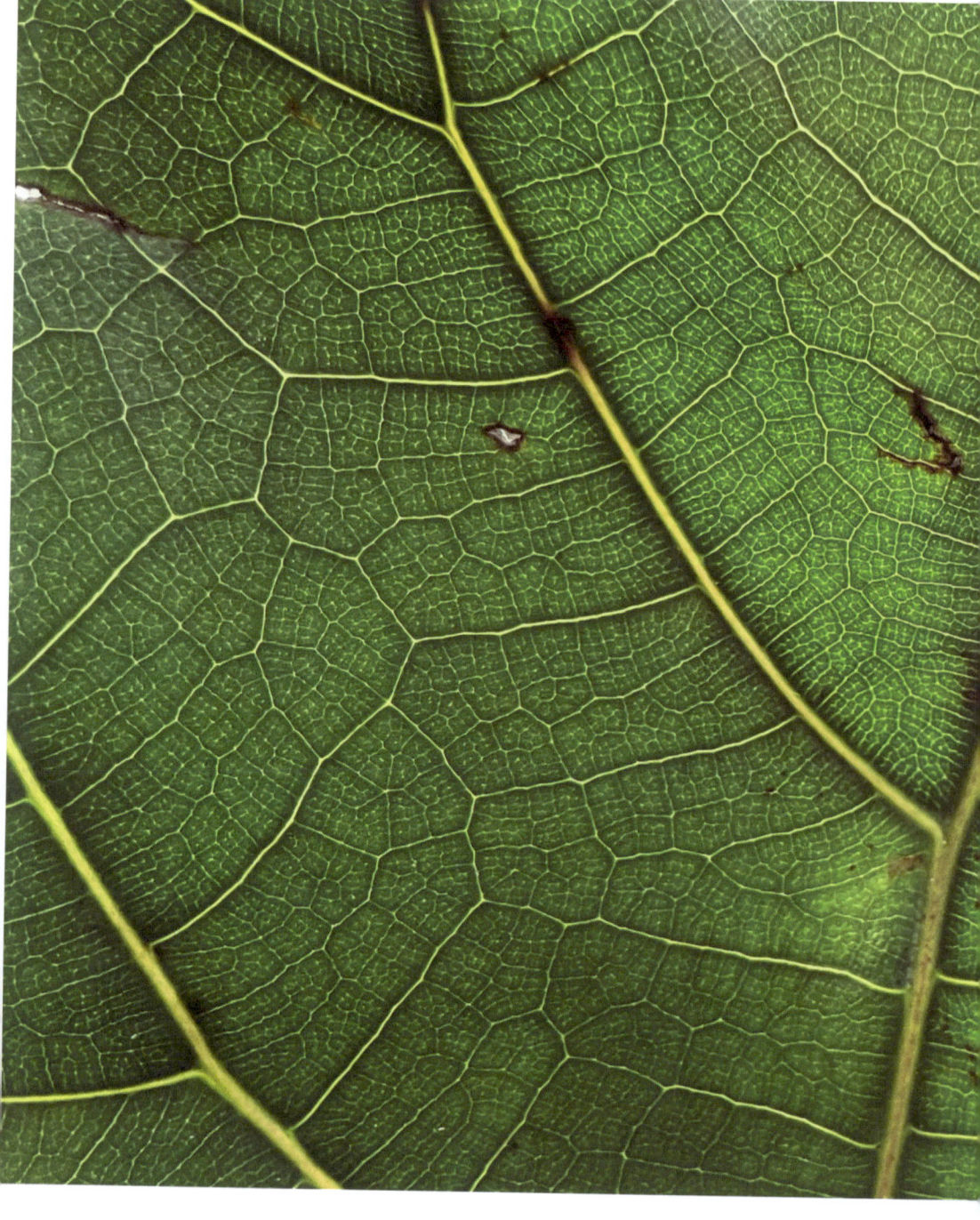

Let Her Live

There you go stabbing old wounds again
It's as if you like the pain
Memories make
When they bleed
As they drip regret
Forming a thick puddle of sorrow

Why don't you let things be?
Leave her alone
Let her live

Don't make it harder than it needs to be
Be happy you experienced a most tender love

Pull this blade you forced into your own heart
Out for good

Let it heal with the good memories you two shared
Let the lessons soften your soul
Love from the scar, not the wound

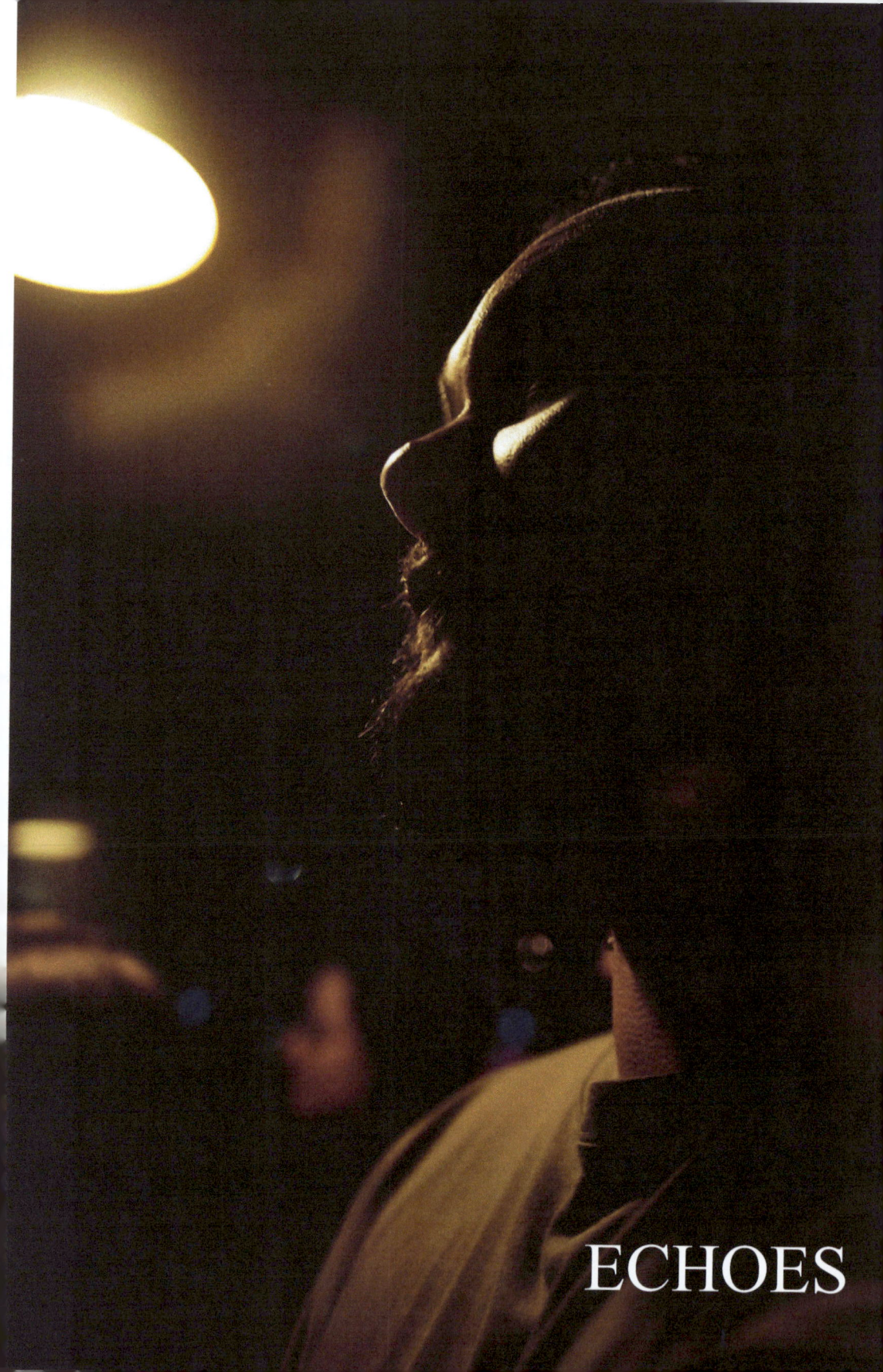

ECHOES

's been 10 days since my fight with depression
 tension
ever breaking, only pulling
ttempting to sculpt out of clay that doesn't have the right consistency
ver pulled by inside forces that pretend to be out

) days
/rap a facade of smiles like drag
Meant for you and for myself
onversation between the echo and its source
Meading with each other
ttempting to convince one another of the truth

0 days
f conversation turned argument
Meated jabs reduced to sarcastic remarks
'm the one who begins
          "I'm so happy I have the friends that I do"
he Echo retorts
          "People tolerate you because they don't want to put in effort to find
          a new person to be with"
choes

0 days
he first 3, arguments, rattling the brain in a quake that shakes everything loose
he next 2 a calm, the serotonin of a faux victory over myself by my self
 of peace, the attempt to move on
he next of realizing I am still in the trap I never left
he last 3 begin the whisper
Echoes
Echoes
Echoes

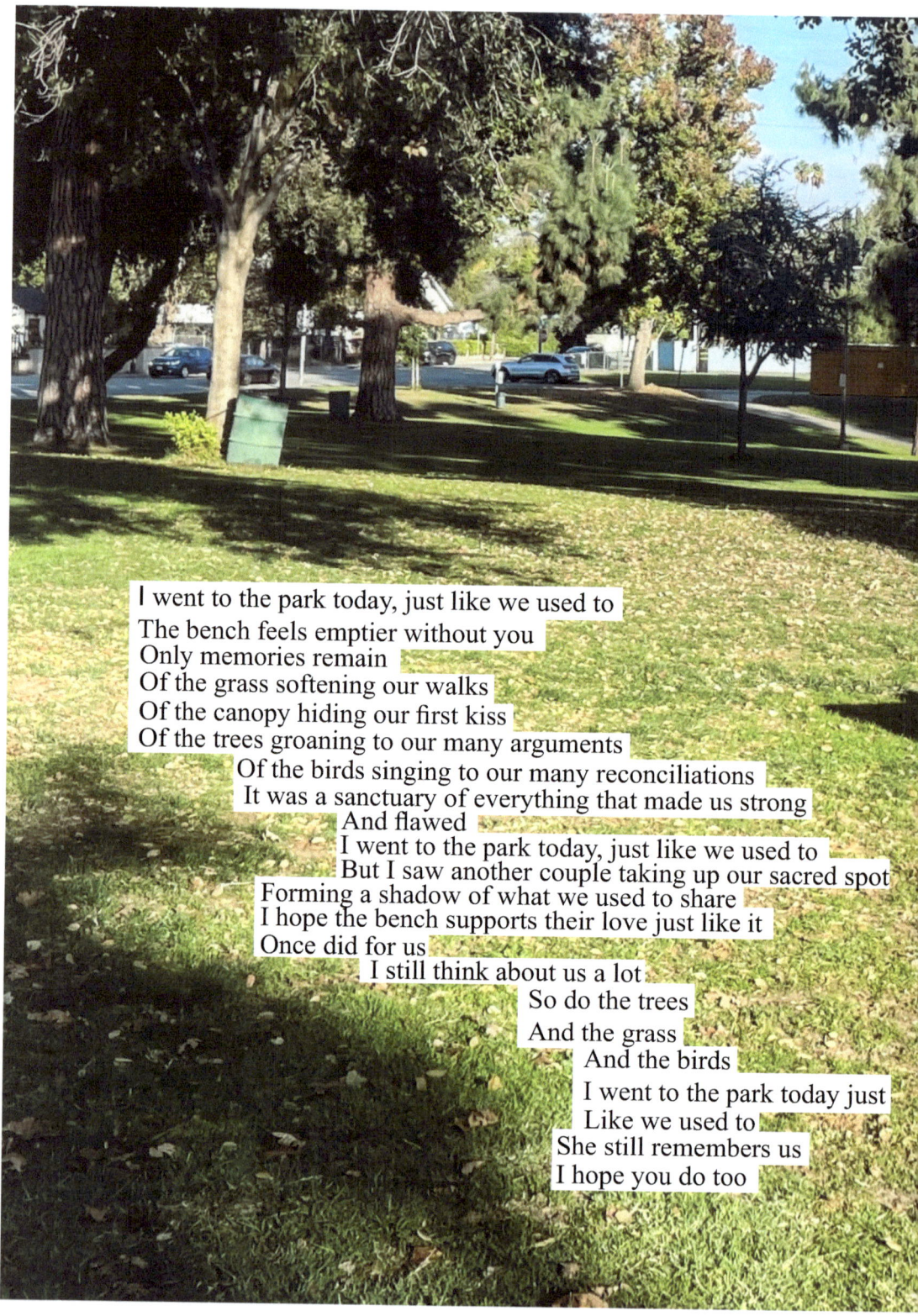

I went to the park today, just like we used to
The bench feels emptier without you
Only memories remain
Of the grass softening our walks
Of the canopy hiding our first kiss
Of the trees groaning to our many arguments
Of the birds singing to our many reconciliations
It was a sanctuary of everything that made us strong
And flawed
I went to the park today, just like we used to
But I saw another couple taking up our sacred spot
Forming a shadow of what we used to share
I hope the bench supports their love just like it
Once did for us
I still think about us a lot
So do the trees
And the grass
And the birds
I went to the park today just
Like we used to
She still remembers us
I hope you do too

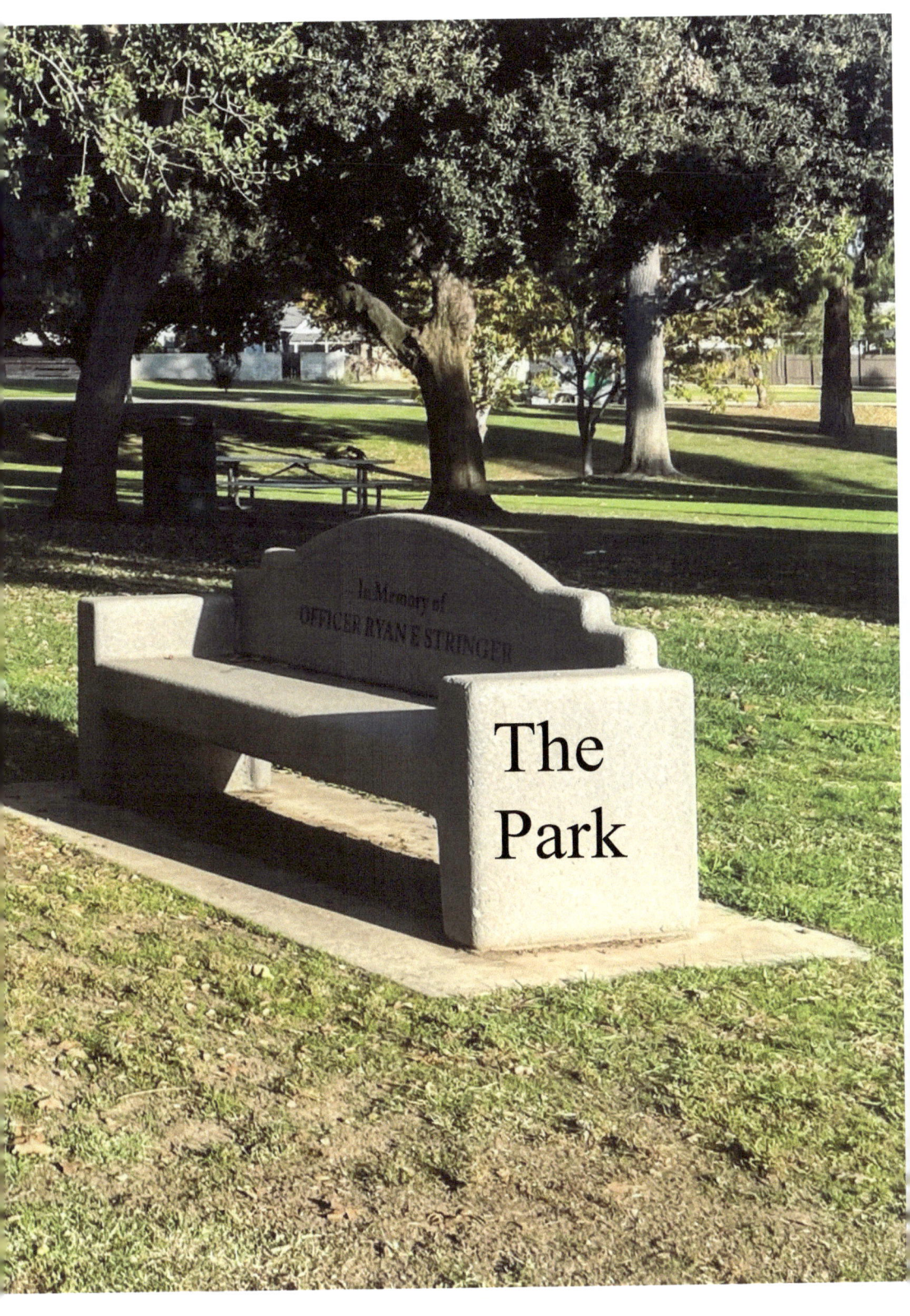

In Memory of
OFFICER RYAN E STRINGER

The
Park

Beats To Fall Asleep To

Introduction

The nightly wails of the dying
Regret to Remorse
Promises to Pleading
Screams of the injured
demand to be heard
Who best to hear than a scholar
Student of pain
Learning to wail

I'm given orders,
unrecognizable
Berated for my ignorance
The language is pain
Indecipherable to me
But I can still hear

Pleading,
Instrument of man
Cacophony,
transformative from harsh
discordance to rhythm

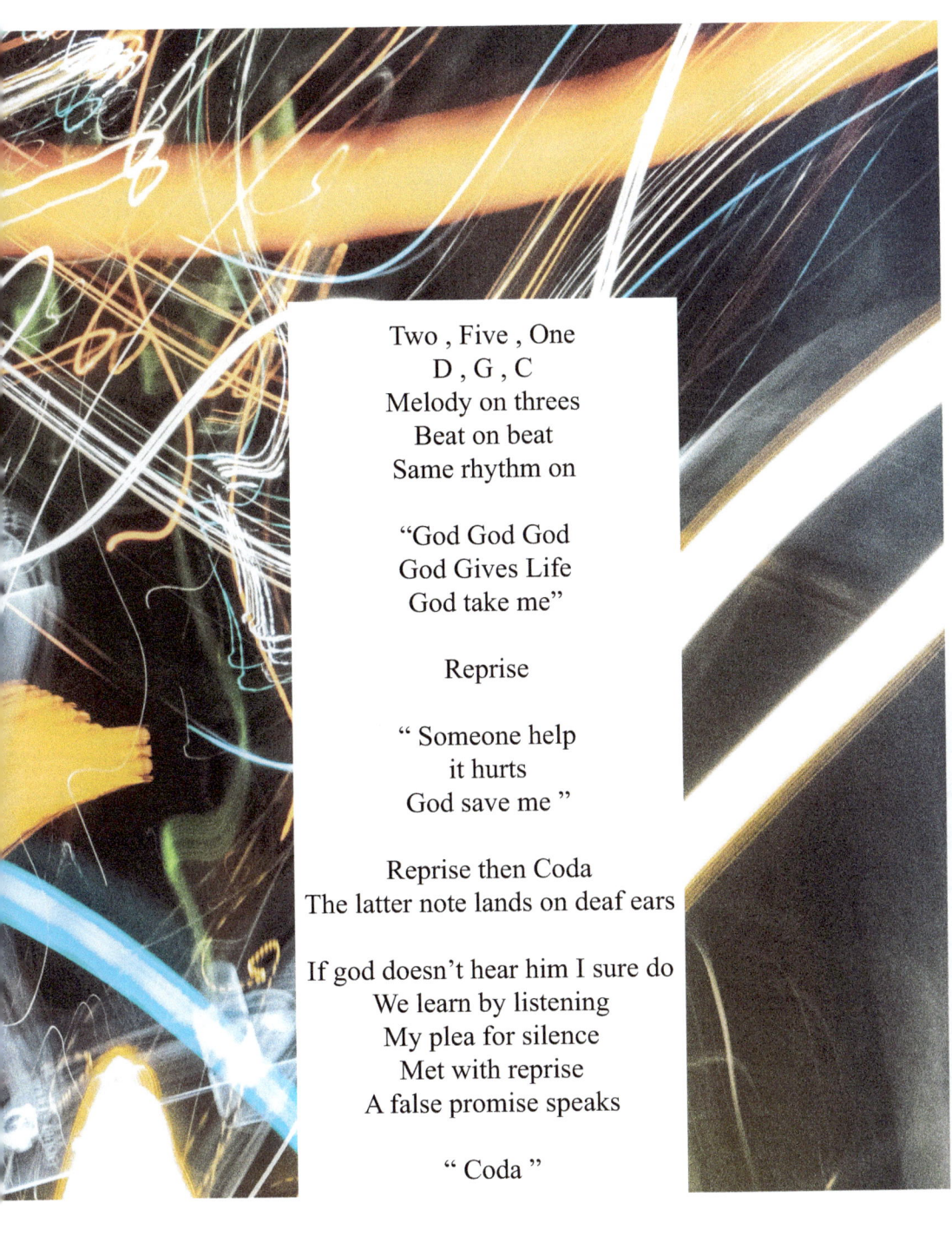

Two , Five , One
D , G , C
Melody on threes
Beat on beat
Same rhythm on

"God God God
God Gives Life
God take me"

Reprise

" Someone help
it hurts
God save me "

Reprise then Coda
The latter note lands on deaf ears

If god doesn't hear him I sure do
We learn by listening
My plea for silence
Met with reprise
A false promise speaks

" Coda "

Becoming

I did something brave
I let go of that toxic job
That uprooted my spirit
That forced me to internalize the
Pain
That made me love like a man
And not like a human being

I wish you could have seen me
Return to myself
I'm happier, healthier, stronger

I wish you could see
How hard I've been working on
Myself
I'm more patient, understanding,
Caring
I wish you could see how much I
Love myself now

That person that held his head up
As high as a sunflower
That person that you used to
Love

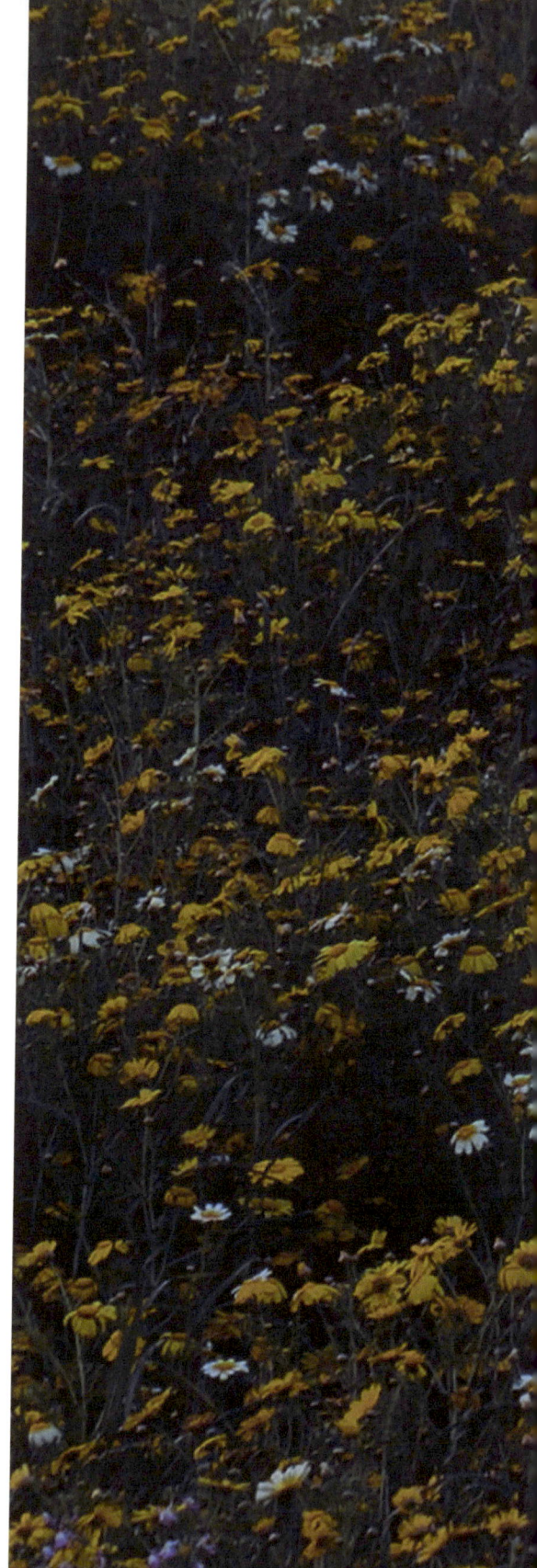

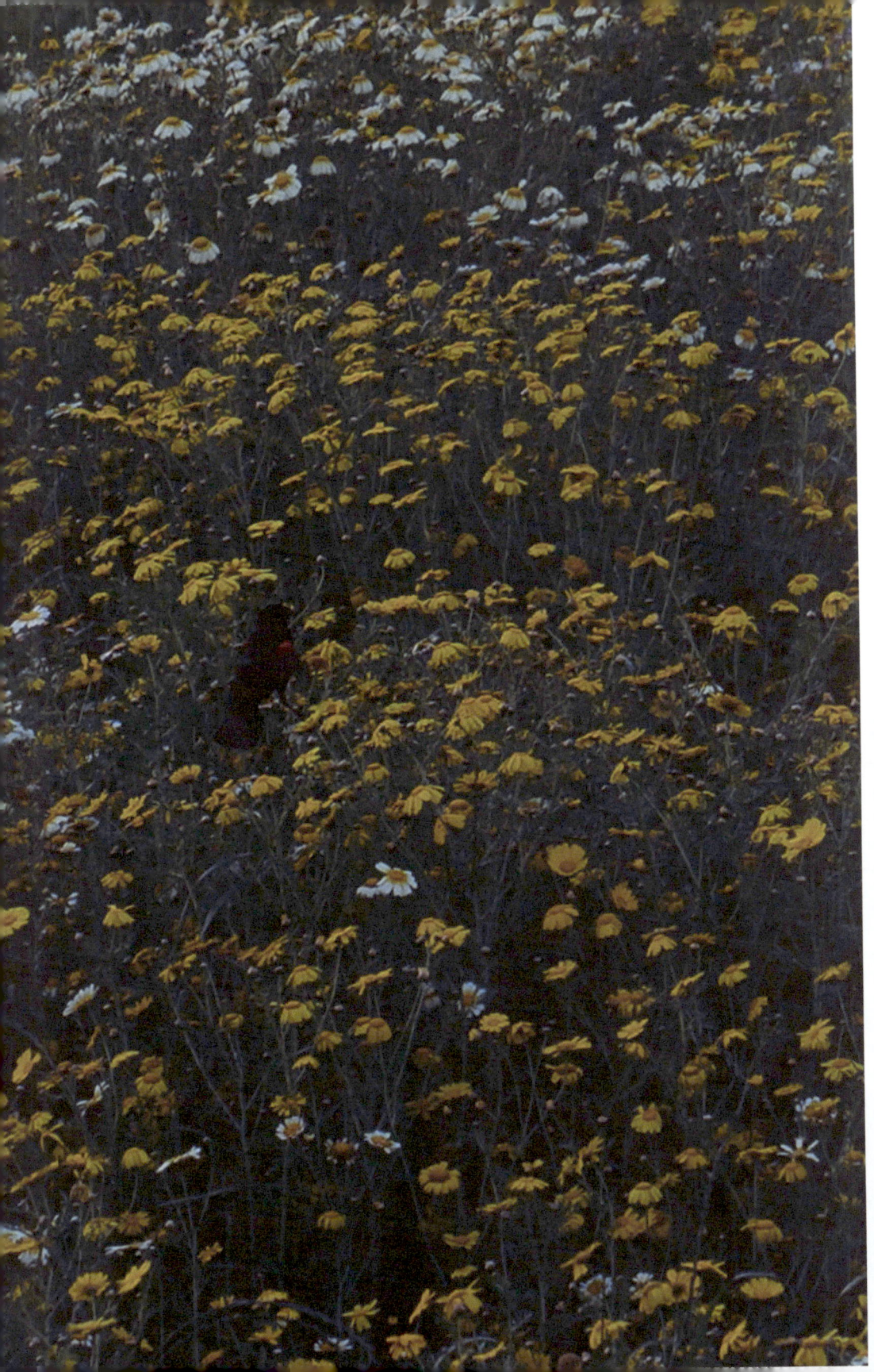

AND THE VERDICT IS

I'm on trial
Surrounded by a jury of my peers
A cabal of those that have been
betrayed

There is no difference

Pleading to the altar of the pity
The tower that those who call me
friend, visit
I am the architect
Drafted these plans in reverence to
my hatred
For what is hatred but one's own
pity,

I protect structure with muck
Toxic and thick, born from my
thoughts

I dig my hands into it,
Coating my creation till it's strong
and terrifying

I am the reflection of me
How disappointing

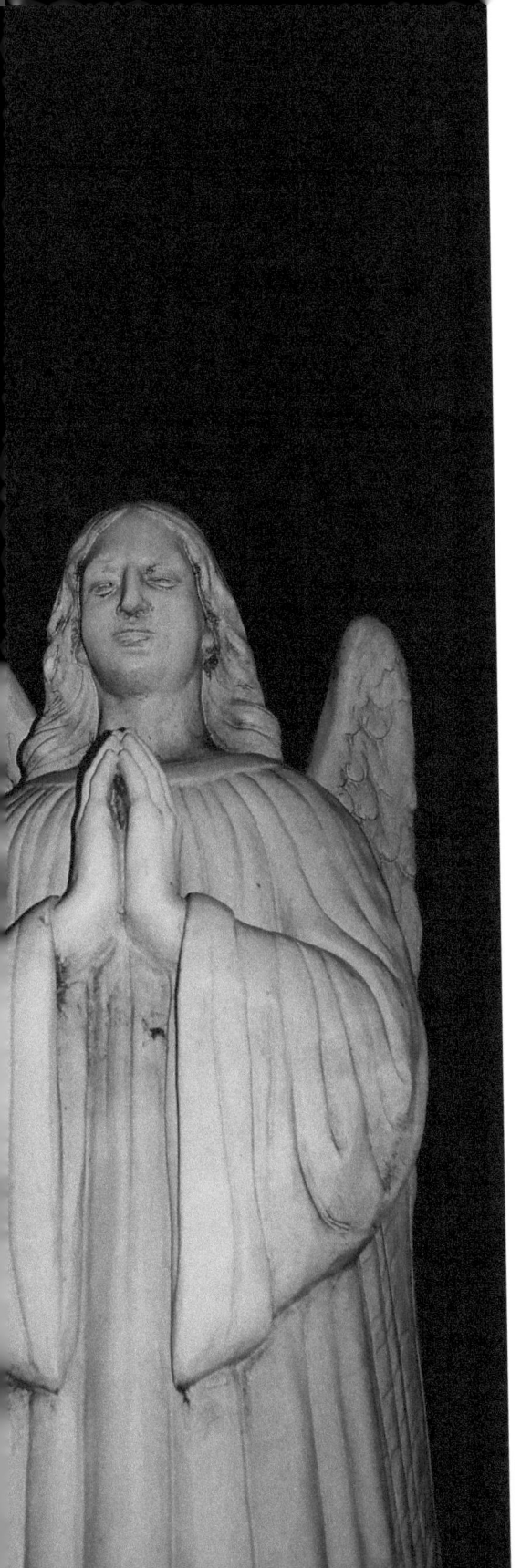

I can't face them
How can I

After I failed to live up to the
visions they construct

How droll it must be
To imagine a good person
Then to be slapped with reality
Each time we meet and depart
To emancipate your thought from
physical

Disappointment is their companion
After their idealism of me is slain
I cannot live up to it

As they cycle in and out of my
tower, singing their praises
Leaving the pews, ready for a
judgment they refuse to dole out

I reach out to pity, my judge
Demanding a sentence that will
never come

For the routine I reside in, is
punishment enough

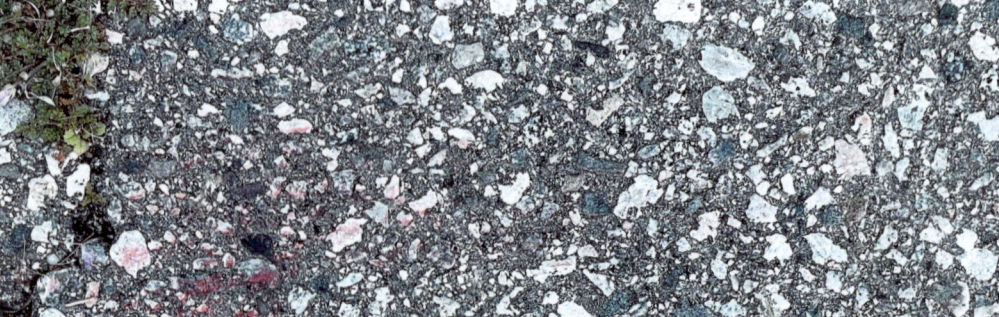

Goodbye Old Friend

I let go of hate today
I thought it meant I had to let go of you altogether

You hurt me
Left me for another

I thought I could never forgive you
I heard you're married now, have a place of your own

And I'm over here still trying to figure myself out

Then, after all these years it hit me
Was I waiting to forgive you, or waiting to forgive myself?

I'm happy for the life you created for yourself
I'm happy for me too

TEXT ME BACK

I dance till my soles are bloody
For you
When the joints lock and beg for respite, I carry on
For you
For I do not remember a time when I was still
When I could stand calm in the wind
Days with peace now abandoned
As your strings stretch across my body
Pulling me onto your stage

These lines bite at my skin
Finding refuge in my muscles, worming around my ligaments
Growing comfortable in my need to please
Letting it feed the strings as they turn to wire
I trace the pain to the source
Greeted by a grinning face
A bog of kindness hiding the muck
behind its fog of smiles
I ask it why
It replies

" Why did you give me strings in the first place "
I don't have an answer
I run away
Breaking the wires
Left them with blood and chunks of me
I, left with metal pokers hanging out
Reminders of the their gift
The pain of friendship
Alongside the gift of departure

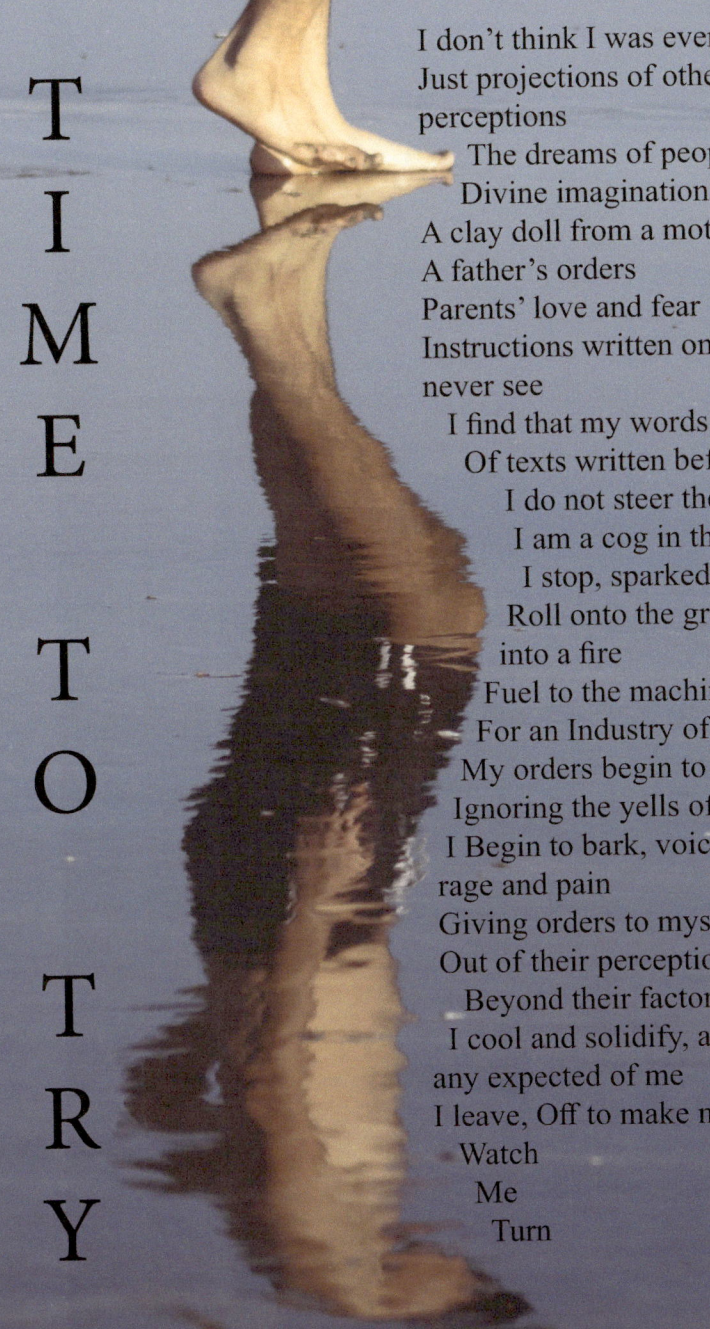

T
I
M
E

T
O

T
R
Y

I don't think I was ever real
Just projections of other's
perceptions
    The dreams of people given shape
    Divine imagination into matter
A clay doll from a mother's hands
A father's orders
Parents' love and fear
Instructions written on my back I can
never see
    I find that my words are copies
    Of texts written before me
        I do not steer the ship
        I am a cog in the machine
        I stop, sparked out of my station
        Roll onto the ground
        into a fire
        Fuel to the machines
        For an Industry of imposition
    My orders begin to melt
    Ignoring the yells of my supervisors
    I Begin to bark, voice mixed with
rage and pain
    Giving orders to myself
    Out of their perception
        Beyond their factories
        I cool and solidify, a new shape unlike
any expected of me
I leave, Off to make my own way
    Watch
        Me
            Turn

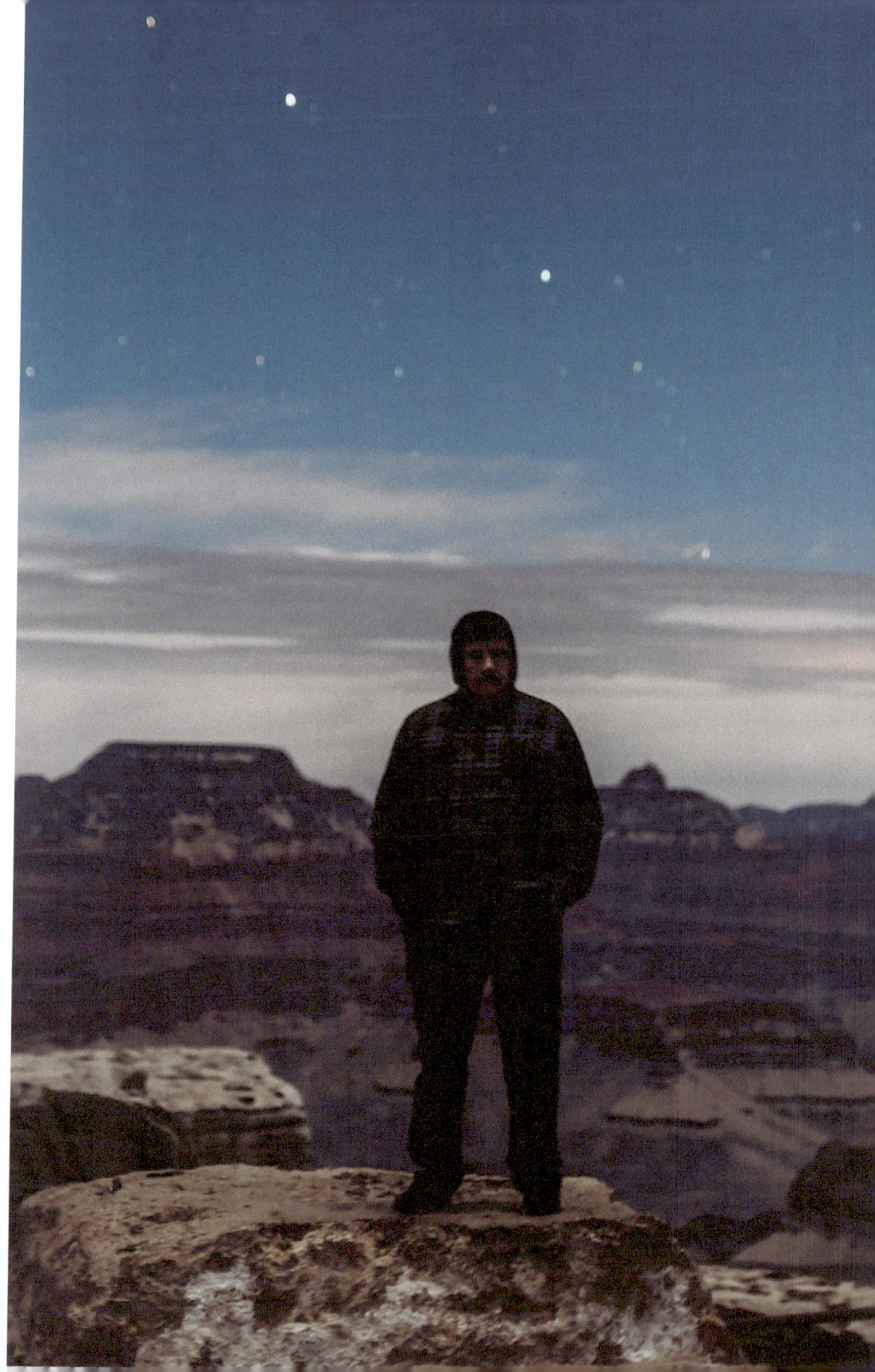

Solus

How can I learn to love you when you are so hard to bear some-
times
Solitude
I loathe your company
Yet I need you
I carry your pain with euphoric sorrow
There are hours you make me push myself away from others
I find myself alone on a distant plane
So wide
So great

I can see the stars as I lay beneath a horizon
But as I try to read the constellations by my lonesome
Comprehend the Incomprehensible
I'd do anything to exchange it for intercourse
Cheap and common place
But I can take no one with me where I am

For loneliness
You have never abandoned me
You are difficult
But that is even more reason why I join you
With wrapped arms
Because when I gaze upon you
I see me
Rejoiced in growth

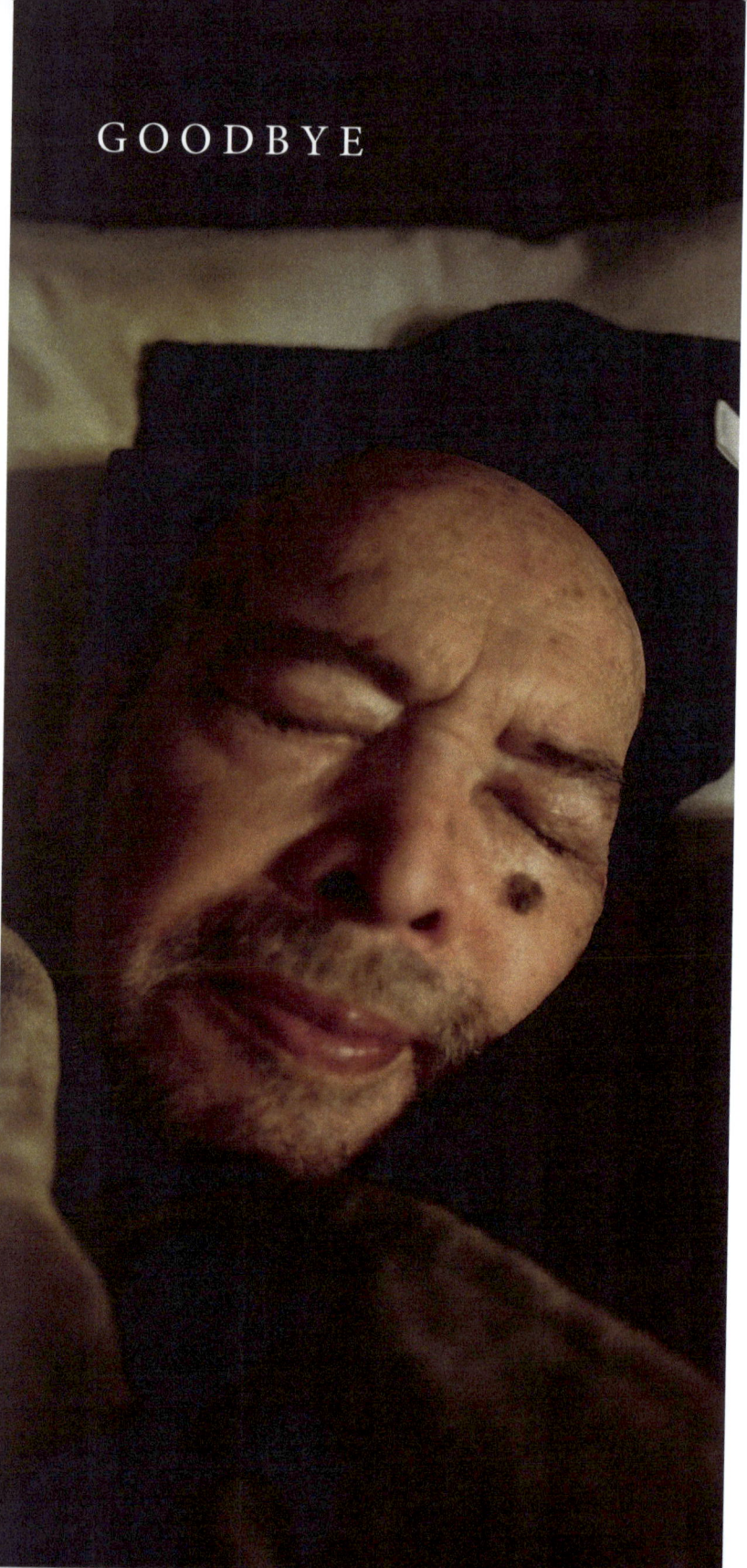

GOODBYE

Most of
my early
memories
are yelling.
Berating for
simple things
Blasé in their
functions.

As a child that's
how
I saw it.
Sermons of his
adjudication.
Pushing his truth
, his
wisdom
upon me.

Like many, I was
his
sidekick for a
time.
A bit player who
was there to
listen.
To the small
tidbits of his life.

To the dead
silence that told
me more about
what he did not
want to say more
than what he did.

As I grew older I knew those
sermons were not what I thought.

His Judgment turned to wisdom.
His Anger to sadness.
Chastisement to fore-warning.
As I grew strong, he grew weak.
As the universe moved me towards
manhood it ground him down.
As I become taller , his movement
slowed.
His own anger quelled, replaced
with placidity.
Filled with softness.
more dessert.
His grandchildren.
His documentaries.
His random facts about his life and
history.
(which I would never look up
because how could he be wrong).

And then he's gone.
I think it's different for those who
lived with him and have gone
through this before.

We who have lived with the dying
are constantly prepared.
Sleeping like newborn parents.
Waiting to wake up and find our
loved one no longer there.
I had this with my father,
And now with my grandfather.
So to those here I give you my
advice.

My own Sermon.

" When people die , you never
know what they really would've
wanted. People can be
unpredictable. I will not be
thinking " what would Carlos do?
" I will , however, keep in mind
what he stood for. And how I can
live up to that".

He stood for family, and his
willingness to sacrifice it all for
them, even towards his own
detriment. A love he could
never vocalize, but act it out in
the flawed way he knew how.

He stood for perseverance, ever
moving and finding ways to move
past his own failures and traumas,
even if that meant ignoring them.

I will remember what he stood for,
and carry that in my heart.
Add it to my soul, letting it melt
in my rage and heartache for until
it's reduced to the only thing that
is left after someone beloved has
passed.

LOVE

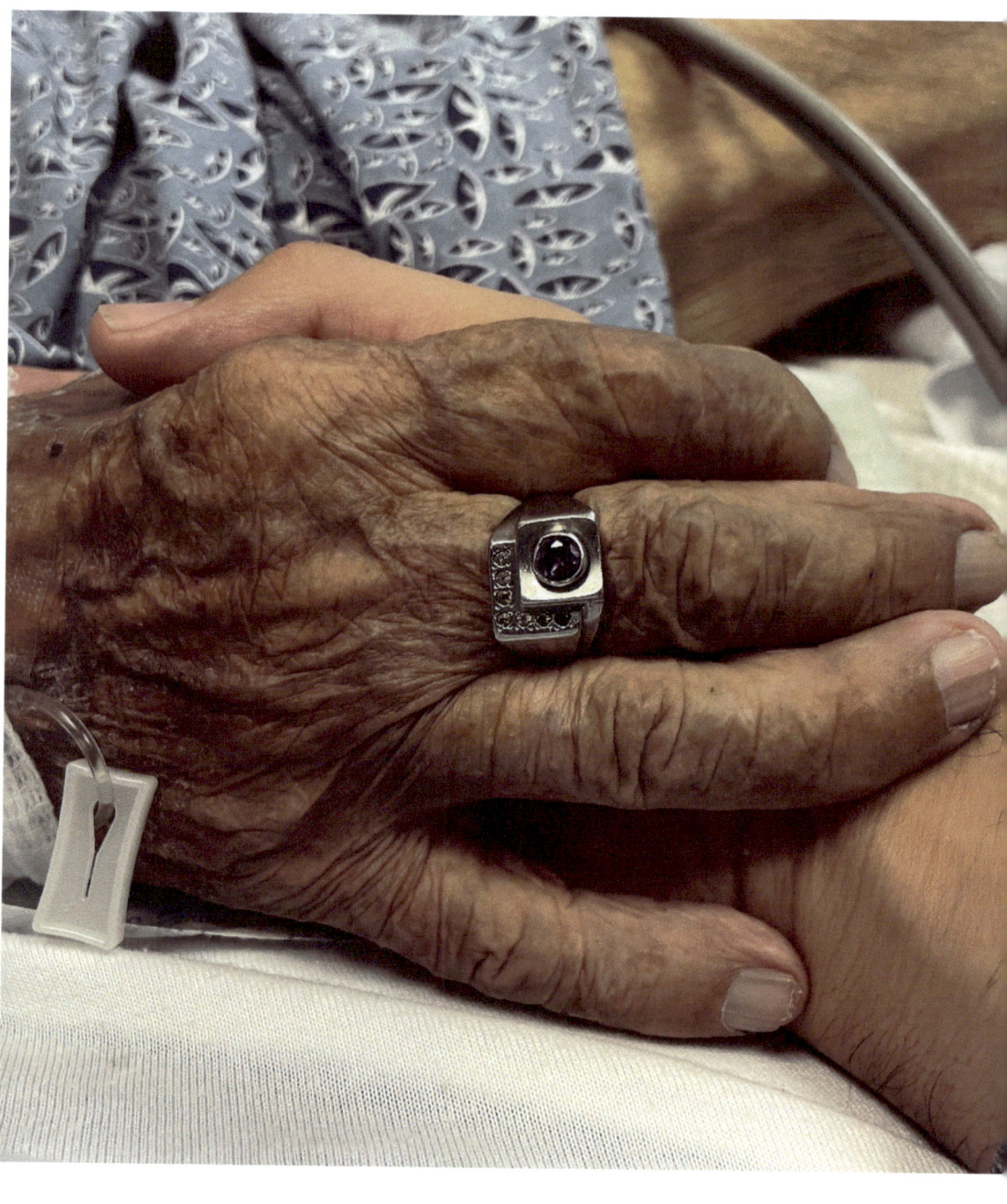

My Grandfather's Hands

I whispered in your ear one last time
'Descanse Abuelo'

You filled these last months with
Emergency room visits
Hard nights on top of the hospital's pullout couch
Waking me up every hour and a half
Accusing us of stealing your immigration papers
Feeding times
Laughter
Worry
Hope
Sorrow
But you know what?
I'd do it all again
Just to hold your warm hands
And listen to one of your stories

Dementia warped your mind
But your hands said it all
You lived a long, hard, beautiful life
I've asked myself
If I didn't quit that job
I probably wouldn't have helped you transition to the Afterlife
And what a heavy gift it was

Is it strange that I love you even more now that you're Gone?
I used to be afraid of death
But you taught me that goodbyes are not the end
The only thing I have to fear rather is an unlived life
Your bravery and spirit now live with me

Your passing has renewed me
To one day have hands like yours
We have made each other whole

LOOK AT HER

I trudge through the harsh sands of adversity
A desert attempting to swallow me whole
Shifting under my feet with millions of rocks
Filed down sediment made of my misery

I reach my hand out for a drink , throat wrapped tight by dehydration
The a drop comes down from the heavens
A drop of liquid that feeds my soul
Moisture tuning down my throat and breathing life into me

She is my water
Life giving and rejuvenating

Her smile, a beam a light breaking through the storm
A cool respite that illuminates my aching body
from the torrential downpour of emotions

Life Giving love that reaches into my soul
Soothing my aches
Balm for the blisters
Kisses for wounds

Then a deep relief off the pressures in my chest
I float free
Breathing deep for the first time in a long time
Her air is life

Filling my lungs with possibilities
Till I'm drunk on her affection
Turning me giddy like I'm gone
Grabbing her hand and gripping it
Lips on mine
Forever pledged to this intoxication

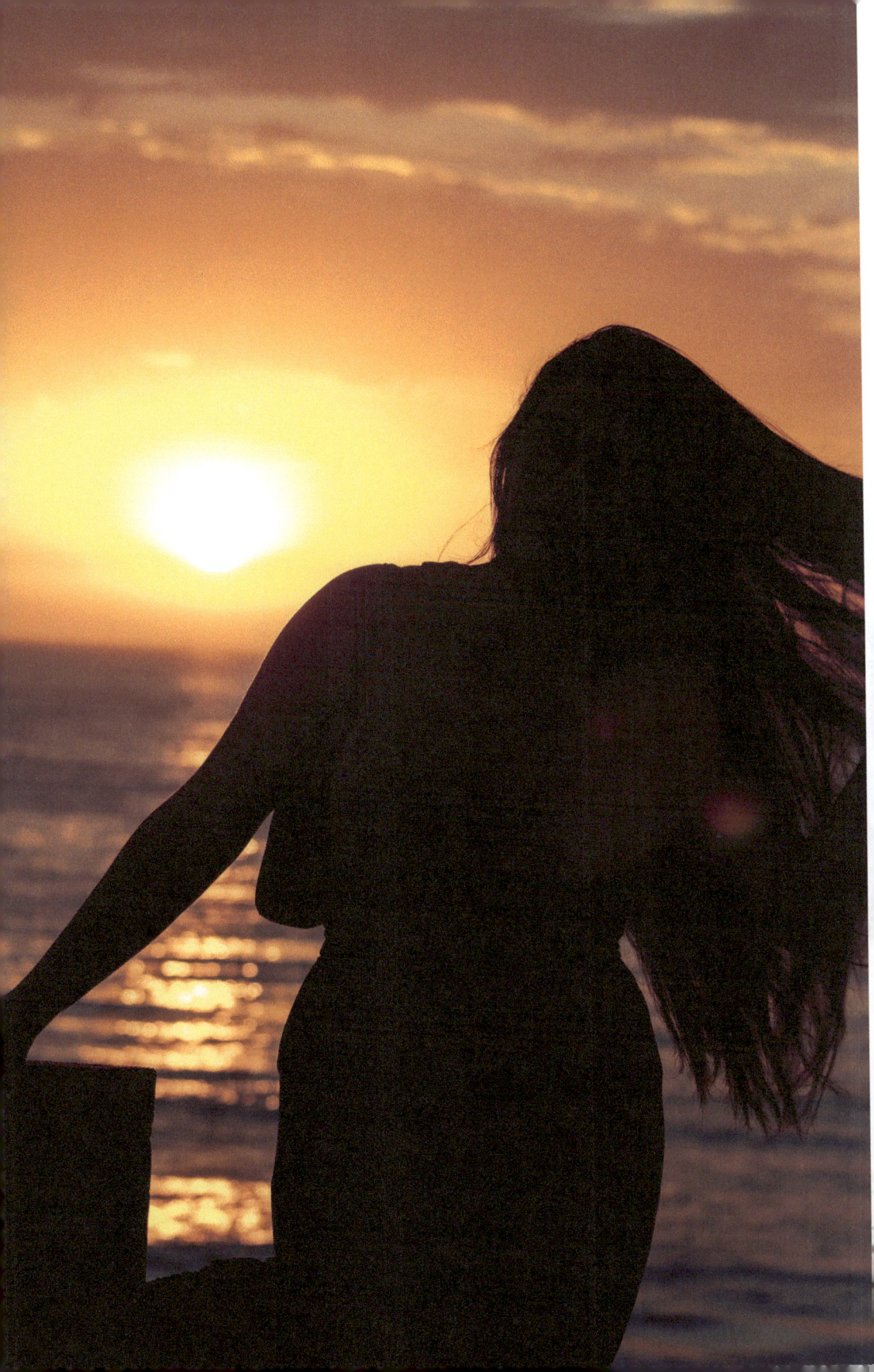

Why Thank You

Thank you

For your

Love
For being loud
For being kind
Thank you for listening
And leaning in

And picking up my Tears

Thank you for being

Vulnerable

Brave

Bold

Thank you for trusting me
To carry your trauma
And your peace
And everything in between

Thank you
For giving me
The will to change
For teaching me
How to heal
How to let go of my machismo
Thank   You
Why thank you

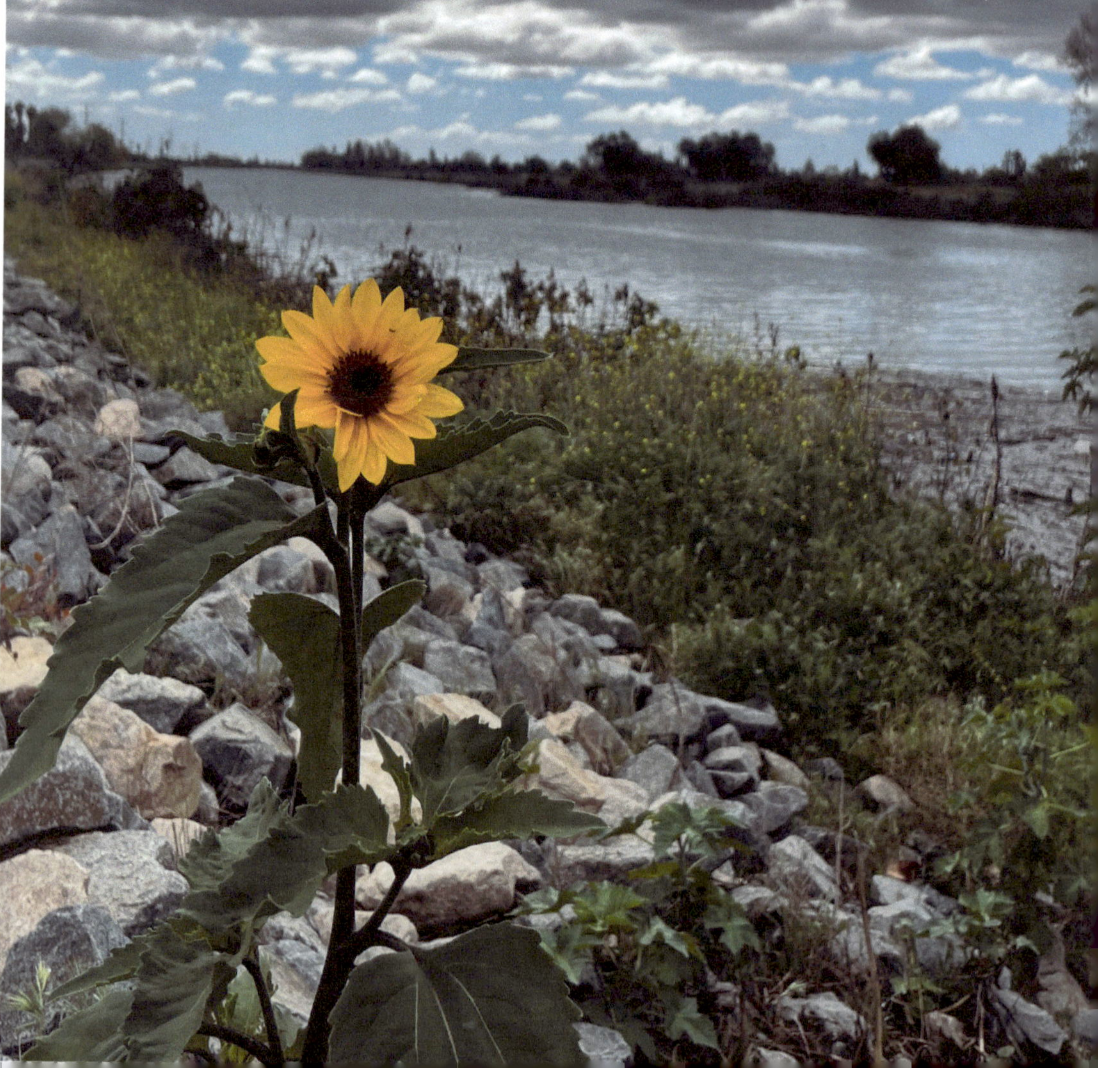

LEAVE

I'm afraid of negative space
Empty canvas
Used to be filled with color
Watered down by the rain
Liquid of change
First of the season
We all move eventually
Pushed by inevitability
Rain comes
And it goes
Yet I hold on
I will not be swept away

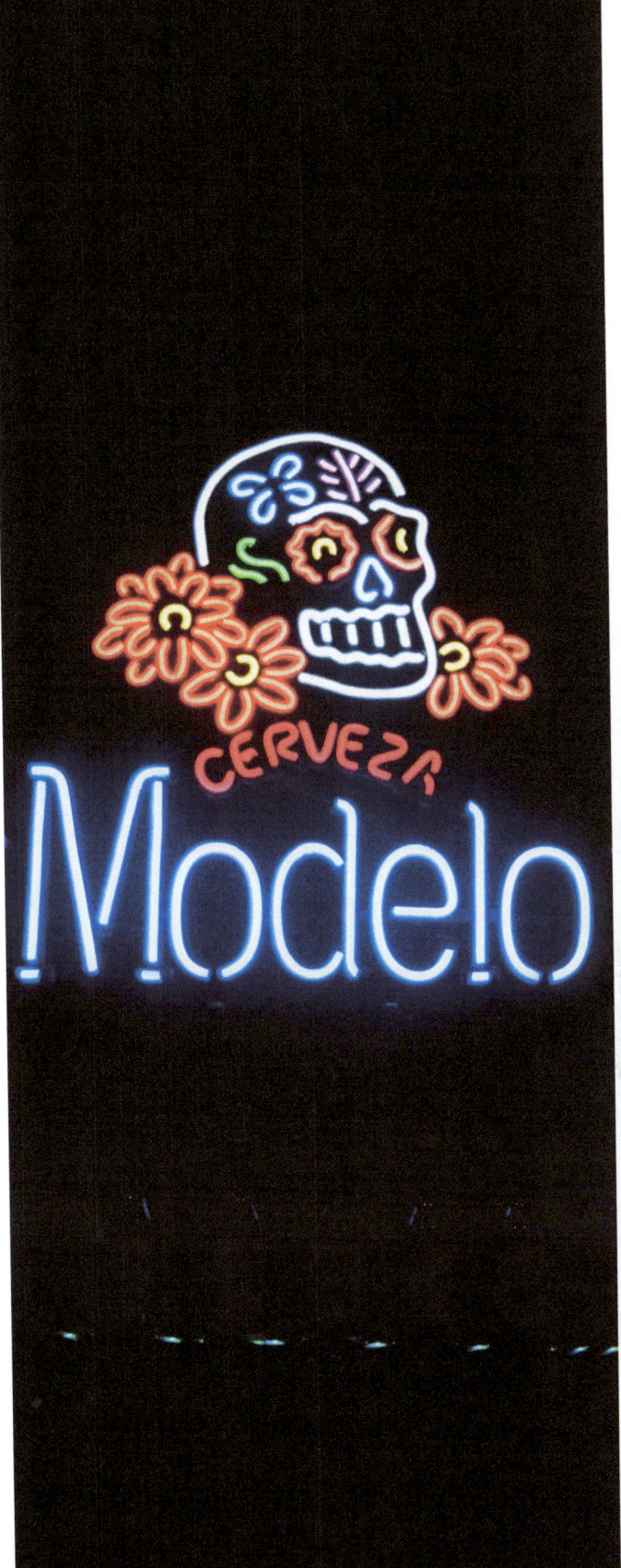

Monarch Mornings

You left as quickly as you arrived
One gray morning
A kind of morning where the clouds matched my mood
But from the corner of my eye you came fluttering in
Bright, With a flicker of fire
Thank you for coloring my day orange
I know you have places to be
But won't you please
Stay a while?
Have a drink?

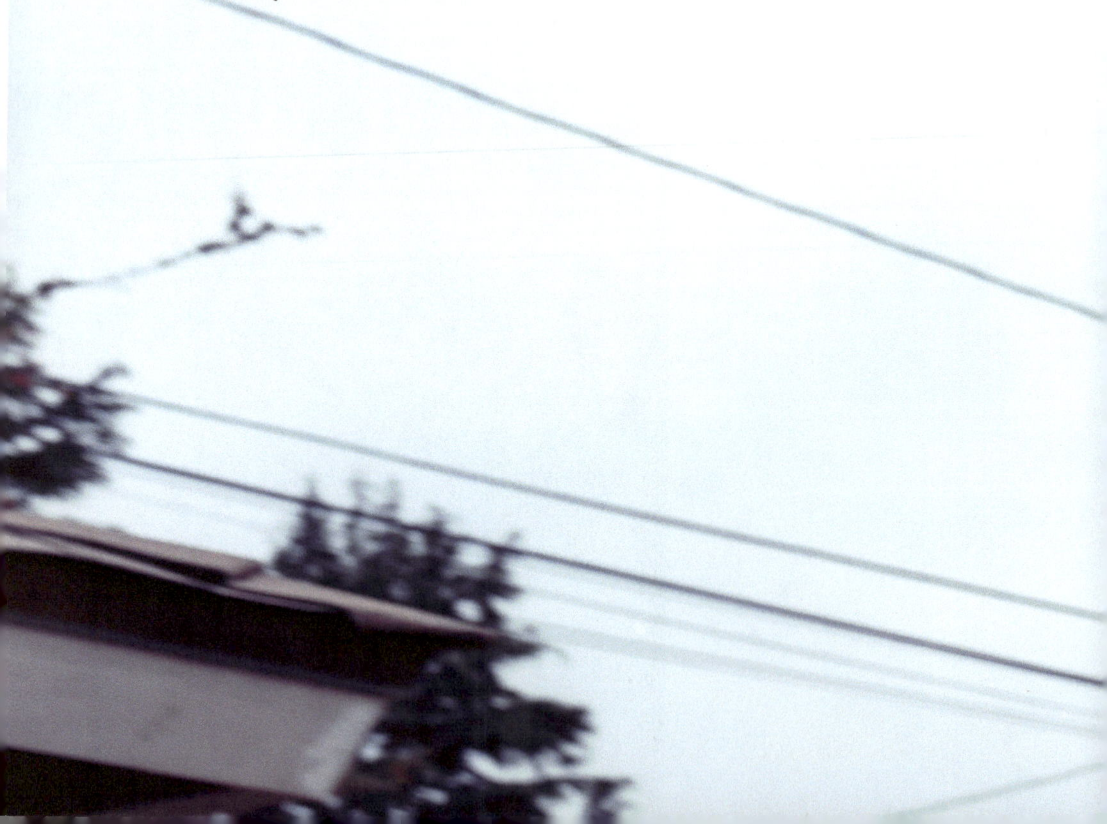

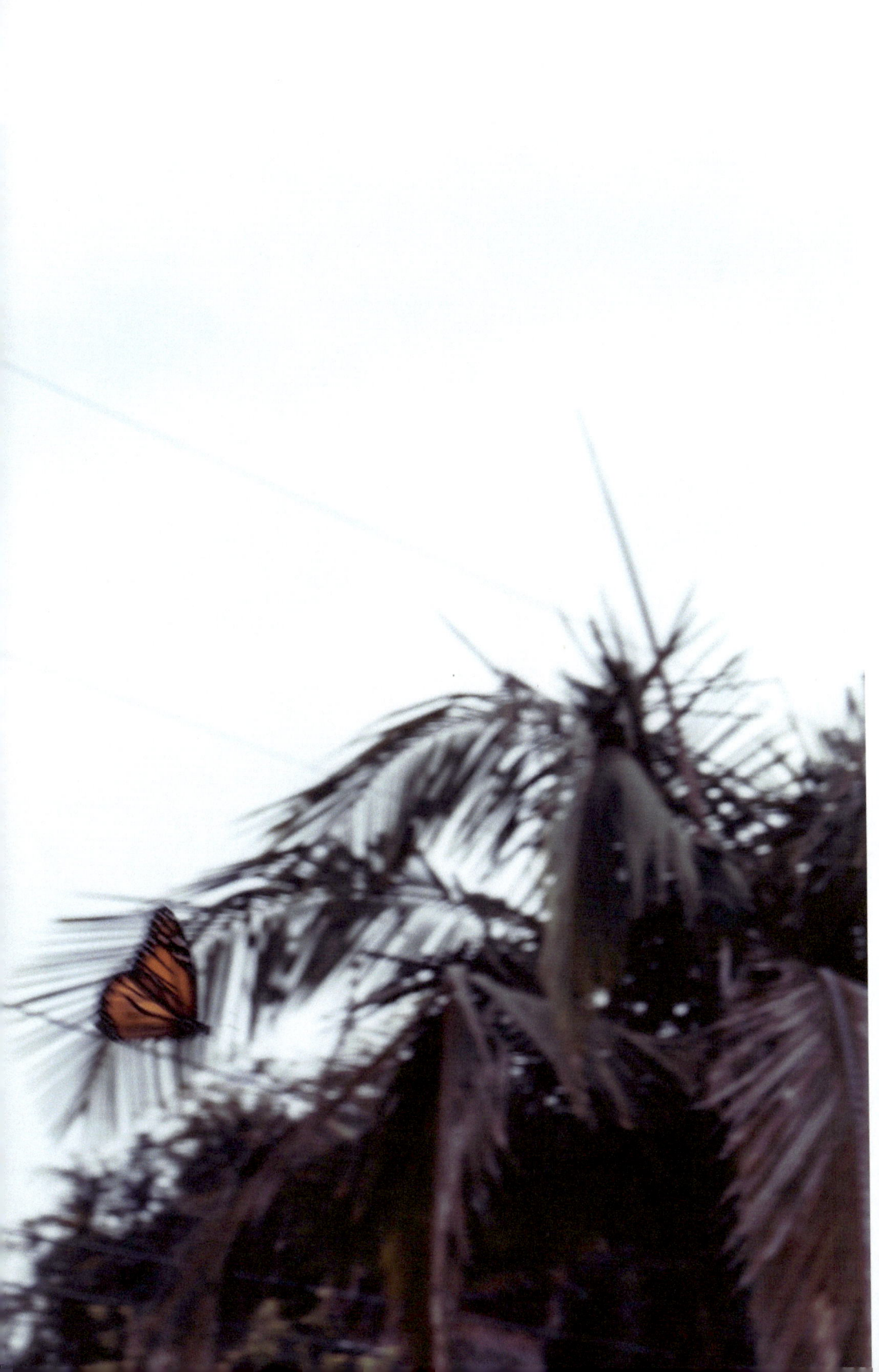

CHOICE

I am what is left
Hate

I teeter on the edge of death
Hands clasped on ridges edge

You watered me with despair
Entering my roots
And I float
Barley attached

Viscous anger
Sustaining me
As a child I was doled out poison
Force feeding me

One hand on my neck,
the other
on my mouth
Choking me on
your indisposition
The brew of vile
hate you concocted

Through years of
existence
It was either die or feed
And I grew strong

I am what you fed me
Bitter
My spirit man sickened
with poison

And now that you lay
dying I can choose
But it's the only
food I've ever known
There's so much
more I could try

But what if I don't like the taste
Sour to sweet
Anger to joy

I raise a hand to
the sky and taste

Sweetened milk born
from tears
Not of anguish
Not of pain
But of something hearty
Something strong
It hits me hard

The pain I've subsided on is light
While this new sensation is heavy
I drink till it's empty
Sinking into the ground
My roots enlarge

Finally anchored in the
here and now
Far more satisfied
Far more quenched
Far more awake

I am what could be

Hope

A Date with a Painting

Oh look at you
A walking masterpiece
Humor as unique as a Picasso
Heart as vivid as a Van Gogh
Compassion as radiant as a Monet
Hair like a brushstroke
Curves of a Greek Statue
Our laughs blended into a tapestry of color
I captured your smile and hung it on the wall of my heart
You left an impression on my soul

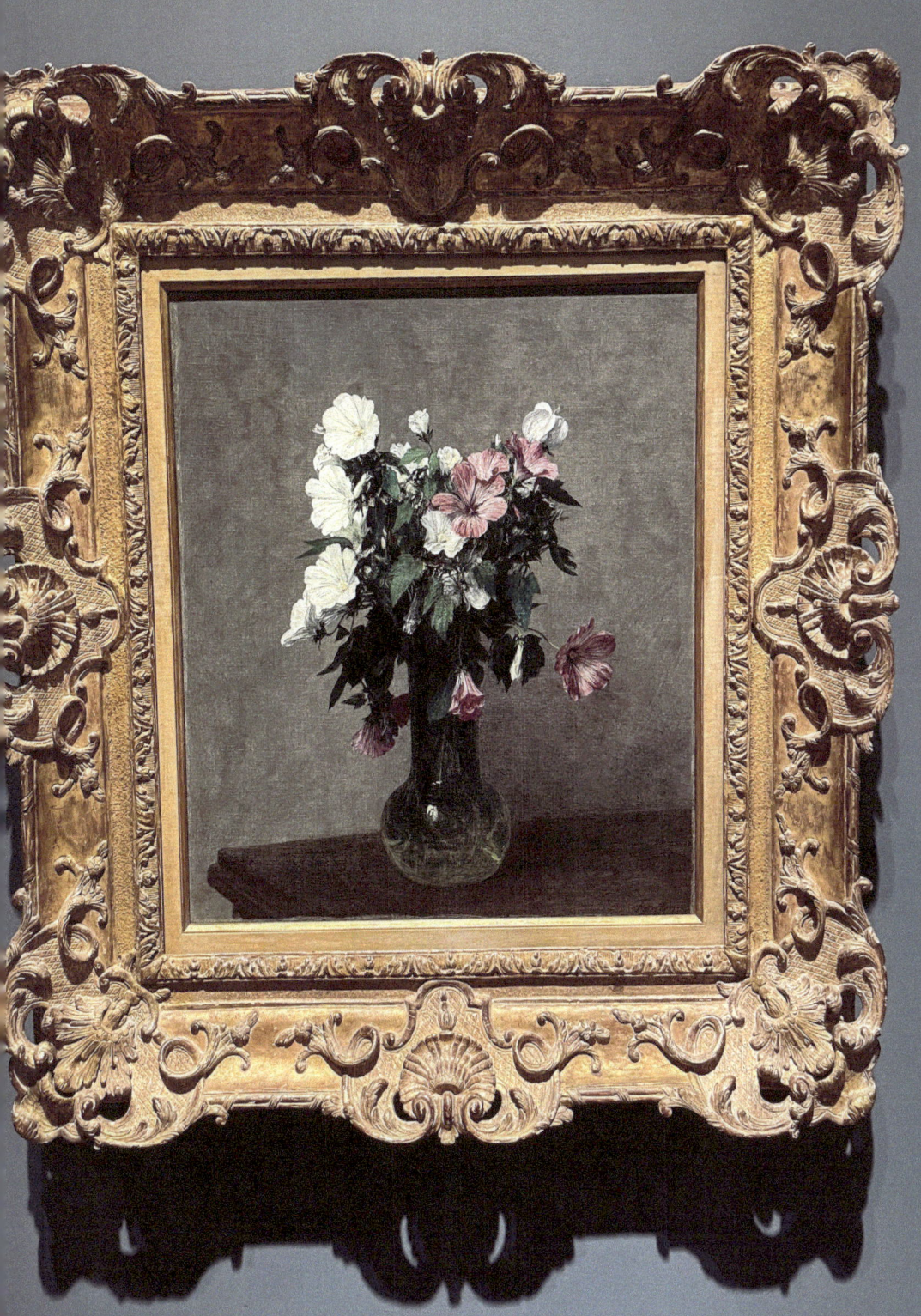

HACIENDA

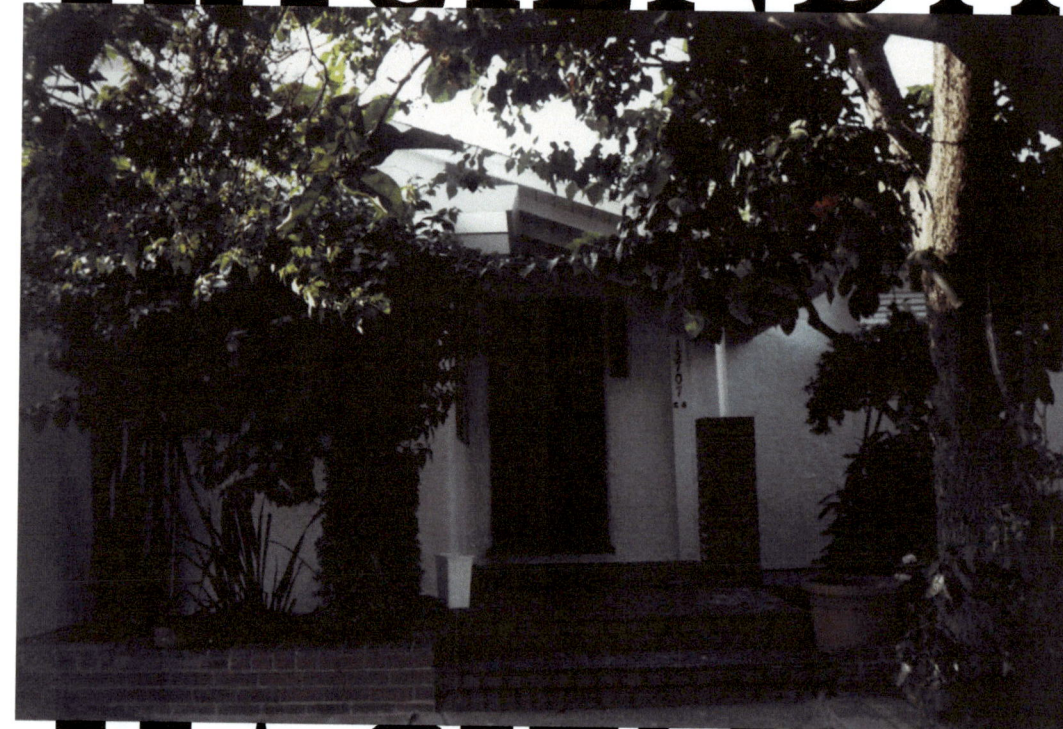

HACIENDA

I'm fake
Bottled up snail oil,
advertised as potions
I smile, rehearsed speech
Going through the motions
Cleaning my space

I'm False but useful
In an enclosure, my home
I am a field worker
Earning my keep
A good life
Traded aspirations for security

The Patrón is dead
His wife moved on
Yet I still tend the field
Selling my concoctions
Liquids that bring dreams
False advertising for a Faux vision
of the future

They say I can leave
I'm free of my contracts
But who will till the soil
I need them
They don't need me anymore

An Inevitability faster
than I realized
I gave my thanks to them
I saw how they built up their homes
Studied their schematics
Learned how they shear their sheep
How they feed the soil
Saw how they treat their lovers
Appreciated how they raised their
flock

Enough is enough
It's time
To find my plot of land
Not a hacienda but a Pueblo
For me by me
One day they'll be room for more
Constructed from bricks, I made

Blueprints, whispered out by my
dreams and hopes

And even if my structure falls,
I will remain standing
Because I know that I can make it
no matter the type of dirt underneath
my feet

Resignación

A lot of our written collection is about grief, loss, guilt.
In English resignation means giving up, quitting, or standing down.
But in Spanish, the meaning is flipped
It means giving in.
Not accepting what things have become
But allowing
So please
Allow me and Noah to share this treasure.
For you.
For us.
For those who are grieving
May we open our hearts
Let our pain pass through us
Transform it into something that doesn't need to be "cured"
But rather something to live with
Something to live for
May we flip the idea of grief into something joyful.
Something beautiful
Always Healing
Always Loving
Always Learning

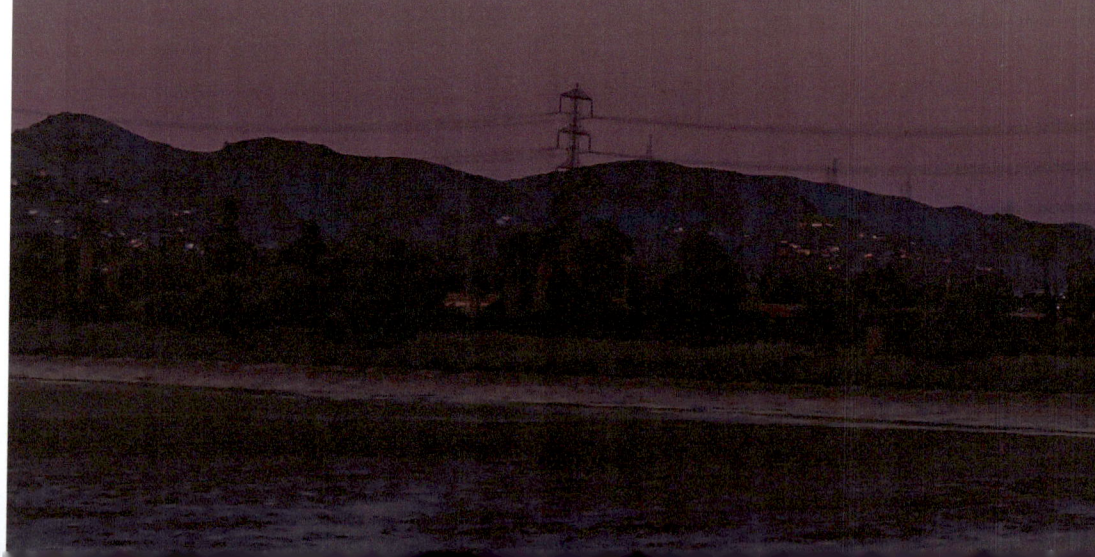

Acknowledgments

Noah Garcia would like to thank his mother (who bought him his first camera) , his friends and family (for all the support). He'd like to thank Wendy Carerra, a huge inspiration and source of strength. He'd like to acknowledge his friend Dazzy, who gifted him the Minolta Film Camera of which many of the images with his poems were taken. Models such as Anselm Krause and Sandra Reyes have been gracious enough to permit their photos to be used in this project.

Why Thank you, Inspired by 'Giving Thanks' preformed Aja Monet, A Date With A Painting, 'White and Pink Mallows in Vase' 1895, Ignance-Hneri-Jean-Theodore Fantin-Latour, Alone Again, Inspired by Letters to a Young Poet by Rainer Maria Rilke, Resignación inspired by AJAAS Memorias Lecture presented by Dr. Christian Bracho. And lastly, my deepest love goes to my Abuelo Rudy, who passed away May 31st 2024.

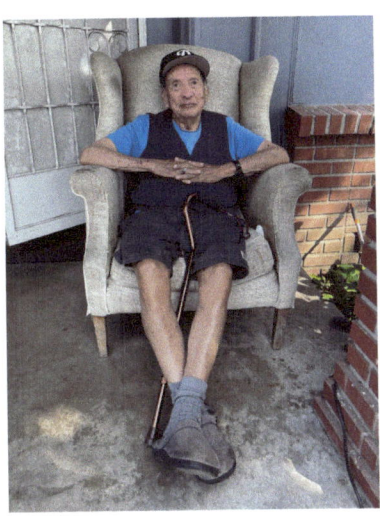

About The Authors

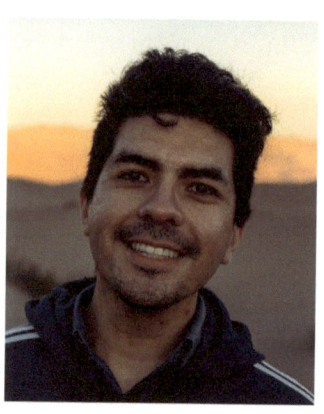

Rudy Juarez-Pinedo graduated from Rio Hondo College, Chapman University, and most recently completed his Master's at CSULA. His family has called LA County home since his parents immigrated to Southern California.
You can catch him riding his bike down the San Gabriel River, growing his backyard garden, or snapping pictures with loved ones.

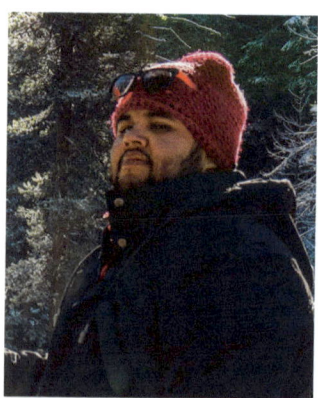

Noah Garcia is a Chicano writer, photographer, reader, and embracer of chaos. He is a graduate of Rio Hondo Community College and CSU Long Beach.
His works have been published - both in print and digitally- through : El Paisano Media, CSULBs' News program Beach TV and the Daily 49er.
When he's not writing poetry or shooting with his trusty camera, he's either reading or working on plans for his Dungeons and Dragons group.

This Art-book was created by Rodolfo Juarez Pinedo and Noah Garcia. The photos were taken, the poetry was written and was edited by said creators. Further editing was done by Diana Juarez

www.ingramcontent.com/pod-product-compliance
Lightning Source LLC
Chambersburg PA
CBHW040759240526
45474CB00008B/117